THE ROSE GARDEN

Old-Fashioned Roses

ELVIN McDONALD

THE ROSE GARDEN

Old-Fashioned Roses

SMITHMARK

ELVIN McDONALD

This edition published by Smithmark Publishers, a division of U.S. Media Holdings, Inc., 115 West 18th Street, New York, NY 10011.

Smithmark books are available for bulk purchase for sales promotion and premium use. For details, write or call the manager of special sales, Smithmark Publishers, 115 West 18th Street, New York, NY 10011.

TEXT & PHOTOGRAPHY: Elvin McDonald
DESIGN: Stephen Fay
SERIES EDITOR: Kristen Schilo, Gato & Maui Productions

Printed and bound in Hong Kong

10 9 8 7 6 5 4 3 2 1

ISBN: 0-7651-9065-5

McDonald, Elvin.
        Old-fashioned roses / Elvin McDonald.
        p. cm. — (Rose garden series)
        ISBN 0-7651-9065-6 (alk. paper)
        1. Old roses.   I. Title.   II. Series:
        McDonald, Elvin. Rose garden series.
    SB411.65.O55M44   1998
    635.9´33734–dc21
                                            98-29135
                                            CIP

DEDICATION

Margaret Sharpe
Rosemary Sims
The Rose Rustlers

*Thanks especially
to Carol Hendrick of Brenham, Texas,
for helping edit the pictures at the outset,
to Hilary Winkler of San Francisco,
my research assistant,
who helped sort the words at the end,
to Dave Kvitne,
who actually dug the beds
and planted the roses in my garden...
and
to the gardeners
who permitted me to photograph
in their gardens...*

✷

Old-Fashioned Roses and its three sibling books from *The Rose Garden* series, *Tea Roses, Climbing Roses,* and *Shrub Roses,* have their beginnings in the first rose I planted at age five, about fifty-five years ago, but most specifically in the season (1985) when it was my privilege to work for days and weeks alongside world-class rosarian Stephen Scanniello in the Cranford Rose Garden at the Brooklyn Botanic Garden. Later, I grew and sold roses in Houston, Texas, and I am now in the process of planting my own rose garden in West Des Moines, Iowa. Book teammates, publisher Marta Hallett, series editor Kristen Schilo, and designer Stephen Fay, helped make my *Color Garden* series, *Red, White, Blue,* and *Yellow,* an international success. *The Rose Garden* series is written in the same spirit, to say the big things about a complex subject in a small book.

Contents

Really Old

THERE IS EVIDENCE THAT THE ROSE predates the human race, and historically roses have been cultivated for hundreds of years. They were cherished in China and Europe long before they were united at the beginning of the 19th century.

The arrival in Europe of the four Chinese "stud" roses that carried with them the precious genes for remontancy—everblooming habit—would forever change the world of roses. The four include *Rosa chinensis* 'Semperflorens' (1792) or Slater's

Crimson China, Parsons' Pink China (a hybrid between *R. chinensis* and *R. odorata* 'Gigantea,' the tea rose), Humes' Blush Tea-scented Rose (1809, also a hybrid between *R. chinensis* and *R. odorata* 'Gigantea,' long misidentified as *R. indica odorata*), and Parks' Yellow Tea-scented Rose (1824) or *R. odorata* 'Ochroleuca.'

A frenzy of rose breeding occurred in the ensuing years and reached another benchmark when 'La France' (1867), the first hybrid tea, was introduced by Guillot, a French nurseryman. It would be 99 years (1966) before the American Rose Society would decree that henceforth, roses in cultivation before 1867 would be called "old," and those thereafter, "modern."

AT LEFT & FAR
LEFT: Found in
1765, the original
wild Irish rose, *Rosa*
x *hibernica*, is a nat-
ural hybrid between
R. pimpinellifolia
and *R. canina*; some
clones may be
remontant.

Really Old

A group in Texas, known as the Rose Rustlers, a name more swashbuckling than its actual members, has been credited with rekindling interest in old roses. The "Rustlers" take cuttings from almost any old rose encountered, but never before obtaining permission of the rightful owner.

Heritage and historical organizations of rose growers have sprung up, populated by members passionate about any old rose, even if it's not technically an "old" rose, but rather a relatively old modern rose. Whether or not the rose being sought is available in commerce is what often qualifies the difference between an old rose and a new rose.

A common thought is that if a rose is single, having only five or at most ten or 12 petals, it must be wild, a species, and therefore old. This is not the case since hundreds of modern rose cultivars are single, hybrid musk 'Ballerina' (1937) and groundcover 'Garden Blanket' (1998) being prime examples. Single-flowered roses have a simplicity about them that makes them especially beautiful in the garden with other flowers and also cut in mixed bouquets.

ABOVE: The stubbled buds of the chestnut rose, *Rosa roxburghii plena*, discovered in China in 1824, resemble chestnut hulls. Primarily, but not exclusively spring-blooming, it makes an outstanding hedge, even in climates given to muggy weather. The crepe-like petals form large, fragrant flowers.

AT LEFT: The richly perfumed *Rosa gallica* 'Sissinghurst Castle' is an old French rose reintroduced in 1947.

COPPER CONDUCTOR

U NTIL PERNET-DUCHER'S *introduction of the hybrid tea 'Soleil d'Or' in 1900, lemon yellow and other bright-to-orange shades that are taken for granted in roses today, were little known. The coppery-red* Rosa foetida bicolor, *also known as the Austrian copper, despite its having been cultivated in the Arab world as early as the 12th century, and another variation of* R. foetida, persiana, *which has cupped, double yellow flowers, are a significant source of these vivid paint box colors.*

The Austrian copper makes a stunning shrub rose that blooms once yearly in late spring or early summer. Since it is rooted historically in such harsh climates as those of Iran and Afghanistan, this is an excellent old rose to plant in poor soil, as long as it is well-drained. The arching canes can grow to shoulder high or more and reach outward to eight feet. They are ideal for training along a tall lattice fence, so that the tips can be bent downward, thus horizontalizing the canes and achieving myriad laterals all along their lengths which will become covered with flowers the following season.

The copper-red buds of Austrian copper look beautiful when the dew is on them and they reflect the early morning light. Later, when they unfurl into two- to three-inch single flowers, their coloration becomes almost luminous when they are viewed with light shining from behind or from the side.

AT RIGHT: *Rosa foetida bicolor* or 'Austrian Copper'; (before 1590); a sport from *R. foetida*; single blossoms are burnished-orange with yellow centers; susceptible to black spot.

AT LEFT: The wild Irish rose, *R.* x *hibernica*, makes a large, carefree shrub. AT RIGHT: 'Old Blush,' also known as 'Parson's Pink' and *R.* x *odor-ata* 'Pallida,' was discovered in China in 1789. Bounteous fragrance, remon-tancy, and few thorns make it one of the all-time great roses.

Part of the appeal of a truly old rose is knowing that it has survived more than a hundred years, far longer than modern chemicals have been available for the treatment of disease or the control of insects. It is important to recognize that such a rose is truly hardy and will prosper if given half a chance in a modern garden.

It is an altogether more romantic concept, to think that one can cultivate a rose whose very forebears grew for the Empress Josephine at her fabled rose gardens at Malmaison from 1798 to 1814. Theophrastus asked early in the third century B.C. that we consider how the torch of life is passed from plant to plant through the medium of small cuttings. Roses for Josephine's garden were passed from England to France by special envoy when the two countries were at war.

True old roses more loved now than even in their earlier heydays include: 'Quatre Saisons' or Autumn Damask (before 1819), Complicata (gallica, date unknown), 'Fantin Latour' (centifolia, date unknown), 'Felicité Parmentier' (Alba, 1834), 'Kazanlik' (Damask, 1850), 'Madame Plantier' (Alba, 1835), and *R. damascena versicolor* (Damask, pre-1551). Not only are they great performers, there is no denying the charm contained within a rose reborn every season for a century or more.

Sampler

OLD GARDEN ROSES ARE AT THEIR BEST in cottage-style and country gardens. The cottage influence suggests that they may be grown in beds with companions as far-reaching as vegetables, herbs, fruits, berries, flowers, ornamental shrubs, and all manner of flowering vines. Passionate old rose collectors are happiest when they find a survivor in a forgotten graveyard dating from the 19th century or even earlier.

Some primary groups from which to choose old roses include the Chinas, the rugosas, the Bourbons, the hybrid perpetuals, the albas, the gallicas, the mosses, the centifolias, and the damasks. Breathtaking whites, creams, pale yellows, and a full range of reds from blush pink to near black are

available. Most of these roses have full-petaled blooms that give generously of knee-bending perfume.

If no ground space is available, it is always possible to grow any old rose in a pot or tub at least 15 inches in diameter.

OPPOSITE: 'Etain,' a 19th century rambler, blooms in early summer on canes produced in the previous growing season. The medium-pink flowers, comprised of many rounded petals, yield a light fragrance. **AT LEFT:** Pale, blush-pink 'Stanwell Perpetual' is a hybrid perpetual dating from 1838. A long flowering season and generous fragrance make it a perennial favorite.

17

Sampler

AT LEFT: 'Baronne Prevost,' a hybrid perpetual, was introduced by Desprez of France in 1841. It continues to be cultivated and cherished for its fragrant, dark rose-pink blossoms. Its main flowering in early summer, followed by a welcome fall show, make it a wonderful rose for bouquets.

AT RIGHT: 'Lady Hillingdon' is a strongly fragrant, relatively thornless, 1910 tea rose from Lowe and Shawyer of the United Kingdom.

A great tea rose that has survived the test of time is 'Climbing Lady Hillingdon,' a sport discovered by Hicks of the United Kingdom in 1917. Its enthusiastic, plum-colored canes grow 15 to 20 feet and are set with lustrous, leathery leaves. It should be awarded five stars for its remontancy, intoxicating fragrance, and long-lasting qualities as a bouquet rose. If you live in a mildly cold climate, coddle it against a warm wall. If your garden suffers temperatures below 0°F., be content to visit 'Climbing Lady Hillingdon' when you go south.

'Clotilde Soupert' was introduced by Soupert and Notting in Luxembourg in 1890. From a cross of 'Mignonette' by 'Mme. Damaizin,' it represents that now elusive class of small-flowered, bush roses known as polyantha. These were the most popular bedding roses from the beginning of the 20th century until the onset of World War II. Individual flowers of 'Clotilde Soupert' can measure to nearly three inches across and are comprised of many rounded petals that lightly incurve in the manner of a big, fluffy, double peony. They give generously of old rose fragrance and appear constantly from early summer until a killing frost.

'Mignonette,' introduced by the Guillot Brothers of France in 1880, has big clusters of small, globular, blush-pink flowers. It grows to knee high and may be the oldest polyantha still in cultivation for today's gardens.

One of the earliest miniature roses still available is 'Rouletii,' from *Rosa chinensis minima*. Discovered growing in a window box in Switzerland in 1918, it has small, dark pink flowers that are solitary or clustered, and is sometimes offered in seed form for a yield of seedlings that bloom in their first season.

Although the 'Rouletii' is generally accepted as the earliest miniature rose to be grown in the West, its forebears probably were cultivated in China long before the seeds reached the West, in all likelihood for several centuries.

PRECEDING PAGES, (left) 'Felicia,' a 1928 hybrid musk from Pemberton of the United Kingdom, blooms continuously even in part shade. 'Paul Neyron,' an 1869 hybrid perpetual from Levet of France, is remontant and very fragrant.

ABOVE: 'Dick Koster,' a 1931 polyantha, is a sport of 'Anneke Koster,' introduced by Koster of Holland. A cluster-flowered, bush rose, it blooms continuously.

RIGHT: Early summer-blooming 'Queen of Denmark,' an 1826 Alba, bears pinker and smaller flowers than most Albas. Its exceptional fragrance earns it a place in the modern rose garden.

24   *Sampler*

PEG O' MY ROSE

ALTHOUGH OLD ROSES *need little pruning other than to remove deadwood and, annually, after three years, the removal to the base of the oldest, flowered canes, some of them do benefit mightily from pegging. According to this training method, the canes of a Bourbon such as 'Georges de Cadonel' (1904) are pulled into a slightly arching horizontal position parallel to the ground and secured about a foot above the surface using twigs or wires bent into long "hair"pins. This horizontalization results in a groundcovering effect and the pro- duction of flowers from every lateral instead of only from the primary tip.*

Self-pegging is a variation, often recommended for new English roses that grow extremely long canes. This amounts to tying down the tip of a new cane to an older, lower one.

AT LEFT & ABOVE: At the Antique Rose Emporium, Brenham, Texas, 90 miles north-west of Houston, a Victorian farmhouse is surrounded by old roses, bush and climbing, flowering all seasons except the dead of winter.

A mark of an old rose is a flower that will be cupped like a rosette rather than having a high, pointed center. Another indication is that when looking directly down into the flower the petals will appear to be grouped in quarters rather than in a single swirling toward a high-centered, formal or exhibition-style flower.

Roses treasured in early European rose gardens include the Albas (white or blush pink flowers and gray-blue-tinted foliage), Centifolias ("cabbage" roses or literally rose of a hundred leaves—meaning petals—that are primarily pink) and their sport, the Mosses (buds thickly covered in fuzz-like prickles with the addition of curious, mossy strands), Damasks (rich in pinks, some whites), and Gallicas (reds galore and ready producers of seed hips).

These early European roses are remarkably cold-hardy and given to a glorious flowering in late spring and early summer. Among these timeless beauties are the blossoms that provided petal-strewn banquet halls for the ancient Romans, the apothecary roses of monastic medicine gardens in the Dark Ages, and the varieties associated with the Wars of the Roses, 1455-1485, namely the white rose of York and the red rose of Lancaster. The pink-and-white "York and Lancaster," *Rosa* x *damascena* 'Versicolor,' celebrated peace.

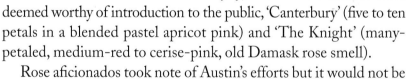

New English

IN THE 1950S, DAVID AUSTIN began working on a new strain of old-appearing roses. Though blessed with the land of his family's farm in Shropshire, England, he must have experienced both elation and despair for it would be the end of the following decade before his work would come to fruition. In 1969, two of his creations were deemed worthy of introduction to the public, 'Canterbury' (five to ten petals in a blended pastel apricot pink) and 'The Knight' (many-petaled, medium-red to cerise-pink, old Damask rose smell).

Rose aficionados took note of Austin's efforts but it would not be until 1983 with the introduction of 'Graham Thomas' (pages 58-59) and 'Mary Rose' (pink, profuse, Damask-like, lightly fragrant) that the world of rose lovers fully awakened. 'Graham Thomas' honors Graham Stuart Thomas, rosarian, writer, and among the first to advocate the cultivation of the old garden roses following World War II. 'Mary Rose' is for Henry VIII's sister, Mary Rose Tudor.

LEFT: 'Eglantyne,' a 1980s David Austin, shows the old-fashioned form and exquisite coloring that have made English roses contemporary classics.
RIGHT: Tea-fragranced 'Claire' (1986) is superb for cutting.

28

ABOVE: 'Wife of Bath' (1969) displays a strong connection to the Gallica or French roses of the 18th century. The myrrh-scented flowers reach to 3 inches across and the thrifty bush can be relied upon for repeat bloom.

It's really no wonder David Austin's new English roses continue to maintain their old-rose personalities. Every so often, in his breeding work, he backcrosses, using true old roses—any in existence before 1867 when the first hybrid, 'La France,' was introduced. From the beginning, it has been Austin's genius to cross old roses with new ones, including hybrid teas, grandifloras, and most notably 'Iceberg,' the hugely popular floribunda.

Since most English roses are remontant and fragrant, they are, quite simply, ideal garden plants. If they have any fault at all, it is for growing over exuberantly. Habit varies from lax or groundcovering to exalted climbing, to 12 feet high and more. Regardless, fountain form is a shared common trait.

Complementary flowering plants not withstanding, hardly anything flatters an English rose like a lattice fence, an arbor, or a garden bench—inviting one to sit and feast the eyes, the nose, and indeed the soul. For all practical purposes, today's new English roses are the embodiment of yesterday's beauties, only stronger, more disease-resistant, and more likely to be everblooming.

LEFT & BELOW: 'The Pilgrim' (1991) has tea scent and is one of the finest, modern yellow roses. Established bushes are more insistently repeat blooming; they can reach to 8 feet tall or more.

English roses have similar cultural needs common to all their clan: a minimum of four hours sun, preferably six or more, compost-enriched, well-drained garden soil, free from the greedy roots of trees and other shrubs, and an abundance of water in their growing season. It is also a good idea not to place the bushes directly against a sun-baked, south-facing wall; allow at least eight to 12 inches of space between to facilitate good air movement.

Although true old roses are usually grown on their own roots, the English cultivars are typically grafted on a rootstock that should help them grow well. 'Dr. Huey,' seen in much of North America is a good example. In the warm Southeast and Southwest, *Rosa* x *fortuniana* will be used and in the far North, *R. multiflora*. They are offered through catalogs as bareroot plants for setting out in early spring or as container-grown specimens at local nurseries throughout the growing season.

Pruning consists of cutting out all dead wood at the beginning of the season; removing the weaker branches that cross and rub against each other; after three years' growth, remove the oldest canes; to control size and shape, remove one-third to one-half of the bush, cutting above an outward-bound bud.

'Gertrude Jekyll' (1986) is one of the most fragrant English roses and its bush one of the strongest. Pegging can increase flowering; one of the best for cutting.

'Brother Cadfael' (1990) is nearly thornless and can make a great rose for pegging or for training as a climber. The exquisitely formed and shaded flowers smell of roses, fruit, and myrrh.

The dark crimson of 'The Prince' (1990) recalls old Bourbon and Gallica roses, as does its full-bodied fragrance. The well-mannered bushes stay under waist height and give repeat bloom.

ABOVE: 'Cottage Rose' (1991) suggests a Damask rose with its sweet-scented, shallow-cupped blooms, produced on thorny stalks with light green leaves; the canes arch from their own weight, thus increasing laterals and flowering.

AT RIGHT: 'The Alexandra Rose' (1992) has the look of an Alba with bounteous clusters of lightly-scented, single blossoms on graceful curving canes, suited to pegging, for a more controlled growth and extra blooms.

NEAR RIGHT: Not yet introduced, this Romantica rose shows its stuff in a California growing field—blooms in all stages and has lots more promising buds. **OPPOSITE:** 'Paris D'Yves St. Laurent' is a 1997 hybrid tea from Meilland, the home of the Romanticas. The large, full blossoms are pink with ruffled petal edges; long stems make it a great rose for cutting.

Romantica

ON THE SUNNY CAP D'ANTIBES, in the South of France, each succeeding generation of the Meilland family has made breakthroughs in rose breeding, beginning with the charismatic beauty 'Peace' in 1946. Recognizing the need for roses that were disease-free and self-cleaning, so as to require neither pesticides nor deadheading, they developed 'Bonica,' the first modern shrub rose to be honored by All-America Rose Selections, in 1987.

At about the same time David Austin's English roses were taking the gardening world by storm, the Meilland's new strain of landscape roses was earning its place in rosedom for carefree bushes designed to bloom nonstop over a long season. Moreover, they could be deployed in public places as colorful groundcovers, hedges, or accent shrubs.

Having created supreme beauty in 'Peace' and self-reliance in many roses, it seemed inevitable the Meillands would marry the two ideals and develop a French expression of the English rose, the Romanticas. Their attributes include old-fashioned fragrance, antique flower forms, rich and varied colorings, different habits from shrub to climber, disease-resistant foliage, and everblooming performance.

37

ABOVE: Romantica 'Abbaye de Cluny' (1998) has large, apricot, cabbage-shaped, spice-scented flowers all season. **ABOVE RIGHT:** Romantica 'Guy de Maupassant' has floribunda habit and smells of green apples.

OPPOSITE BELOW: Romantica 'Colette' is an apricot blend that smells of fruity rose. The dark, leathery, disease-resistant foliage is an asset in the garden and its long stems make 'Colette' a treasure for cutting.

ABOVE: Romantica 'Johann Strauss' grows blush to darker pink roses simultaneously, in sufficient number to enjoy it cut as well as in the garden. It possesses a light, true rose fragrance.

AT LEFT & ABOVE: Romantica 'Toulouse Lautrec' (1996) is a big, many-petaled rose modeled in response to the most vivid fantasies of the glories of old roses no longer extant. This very real rose gives a refreshing lemon scent and grows above bright green foliage, on strong stems that reach to near shoulder height.

OPPOSITE: Spice-scented Romantica 'Traviata' (1998) blooms singly on perfect stems for cutting; disease-resistant bushes to waist height.

While some English roses proved early on that they grow twice or even three times as big in American gardens, the Romanticas have a more controlled growth habit. In general they are also hardier to the climatic extremes of a large continent, where summers can be hotter and winters decidedly colder.

In contrast to David Austin's English roses which offer an outstanding range of gentle pastel colors, the Romanticas are cast in more vivid or complex hues—mauve pink, carmine pink, bright lemon yellow, deep pink, and apricot with yellow highlights, among others.

The idea for Romantica roses began in the 1970s when the Meillands began planning crosses, in search of a luscious old-fashioned flower paired with a bush of robust character to withstand France's climatic variations. They also wanted to produce a full-bodied rose perfume that would emanate from every blossom.

Coincidentally, the House of Meilland is located in the same region as some of the world's foremost perfume makers. Together they have explored the alchemy of essences. 'Yves Piaget' has a "sweet tart" fragrance; 'Guy de Maupassant' smells of 'Granny Smith' apples; 'Toulouse Lautrec' gives the scent of lemon verbena; 'Auguste Renoir' is "sweet"; 'Frédéric Mistral' gives off potent attar of roses fragrance; and 'Abbaye de Cluny' has a spicy, complex old-rose scent.

Because of high petal count and a large number of flowers, the Romanticas will look better in the garden if regularly deadheaded. They make splendid bouquet flowers and the more you cut, the more blooms there'll be.

If space for growing roses is limited to a deck or patio, plant any of the Romanticas in a pot or box at least 15 inches in diameter and of similar depth. Use packaged, all-purpose potting soil and apply timed-release fertilizer pellets for roses. Water generously.

Romantica

PRECEEDING PAGES: California breeder Ralph Moore's cascading miniature (left) and cluster-flowered bush roses offer great promise.

RIGHT: Romantica 'Auguste Renoir' (1998) has powerful scent. BELOW: Hybrid tea 'Yves Piaget' (1989) is deliciously fragrant.

OPPOSITE: Lavender 'Moon Shadow' is a fragrance breakthrough.

Another breeder who has managed to change the way the world views roses is Ralph Moore of Visalia, California. Born at the beginning of the 20th century, Moore said, during his ninety-first year, that he hoped for ten more good years in which to develop the roses already dancing in his head. 'Soft Stripes'—clusters of lightly cupped flowers whose medium pink petals are striped with creamy yellow—is an excellent example of his innovation especially since one of its parents is a miniature, 'Sequoia Gold.' The mixing of miniature rose genes into the rose mainstream could have a profound and surprising effect on all rose futures.

Companions

GIVE ANY OLD ROSE A FLATTERING bedmate and you dramatically increase its beauty quotient. The idea works as well in a patio pot as in a big mixed border—the list of candidates is vast, varied, and globally adaptable. These candidates include other roses, such as the miniatures and climbers, other shrubs, dwarf conifers, hardy perennials, bulbs, annuals, and herbs.

Purple-leaved shrubs flatter red or pink old roses. Consider smoke bush, crimson-leaved barberries, and, as an impressive backdrop, a maple tree such as 'Crimson King.' Among annuals or tender perennials with foliage in this color way are perilla or shiso, coleus, acalypha, castor bean, and *Euphorbia cotinifolia.* 'Palace Purple' heuchera is a dream for playing up all rosy flowers and its tidy habit is perfect for masking any bareness at the bottom of large rosebushes.

White or pink potentillas, also in the rose family, make wonderful companions for red or pink roses. Yellow potentillas and hypericums cast a sunny disposition in the company of yellow, orange, and warm-red roses. Two other rose relatives that can make delightful companions are strawberries and apples, the latter especially if dwarf or trained as espaliers.

AT LEFT: Bourbon rose 'Madame Isaac Pereire' (1881) makes a dramatic backdrop for blue campanulas and catmint, St. John's wort, and hardy geraniums.

FAR LEFT: White English rose 'Winchester Cathedral' never looked more beautiful than behind a dark blue bench in the company of 'Alba' centranthus.

Companions

FAR LEFT, TOP: The strongly scented English rose 'Leander' (1982) is dramatically flattered by the color of *Salvia* x *superba* 'East Friesland.' **FAR LEFT, BOTTOM:** A tidy, hardy, shrub rose such as 'China Doll' will bloom nonstop and makes an amiable bedmate for other plants without romping over them. **NEAR LEFT:** Richly fragrant English rose 'The Reeve' (1979) looks especially beautiful in the company of a red-violet lavatera, also known as miniature hollyhock or *Malva sylvestris*.

PRECEDING PAGES: (left to right) English rose 'Golden Celebration' (1992) blooms behind orange lilies, in front of its family relative, an apple tree. English rose 'Abraham Darby' (1985) is influenced by its juxtaposition against a richly colored perennial lathyrus pea. Red English roses stand out in the company of crimson barberry foliage, in front of an espaliered magnolia, and a blue-painted bench.

RIGHT TOP: *Rosa gallica* var. *officinalis* or apothecary's rose is wonderful in a border with blue bellflowers and veronicas. **BOTTOM:** The same variety as above reveals an unexpected blueness in the company of blue-flowered *Clematis integrifolia*, a herbaceous species that is annually cut in early spring 9 to 18 inches from the ground.

Companions

Silver or gray leaves add to the profound effect of all shrub roses, no matter the color of the flowers. Lavender, artemisia, and lamb's-ears are popular choices that work well in large pots as well as in garden beds. The weeping silver-leaved pear, *Pyrus salicifolia* 'Pendula,' is a connoisseur's delight, a small, ornamental tree of picturesquely graceful habit. In harsh climates there is the Russian olive for silver foliage in a shrub or tree, depending on how it is pruned.

Blue-flowered plants add to the beauty of old roses in all colors. Among the best shrubs are ceanothus, caryopteris, and buddleia. Perennials include Russian sage, veronica, monkshood, delphinium, aster, campanula or bellflower, ladybells, and salvias aplenty: *S.* x *superba* cultivars, *S. uliginosa*, *S. patens*, numerous blue-to-purple expressions of *S. guaranitica*, and the culinary herb *S. officinalis* and its varieties. Annuals offer larkspur, viola, sweet pea, ageratum, and lobelia. There is also a blue-flowered sage, *S. farinacea*, that is treated as an annual and makes a wonderful companion for any rose.

AT LEFT: The idea of grandmother's garden, circa 1900, is no less romantic for the year 2000. Combine pink roses with blue violas and delphiniums, pink-budded, white lilies, and pink potentilla.

AT LEFT: A Bourbon rose blooms at Sissinghurst gardens in England, fronted by a blue *Salvia pratensis.* The boxwood hedging gives structure and welcome winter color. ABOVE: Roses and peonies represent the ultimate in voluptuous garden beauty. After the peony flowers are gone, their lustrous, dark green foliage will hide the leafless lower canes of the rose. AT RIGHT: 'Tour de Malakoff,' a Gallica introduced in 1856 in Luxembourg by Soupert and Notting, blooms in summer and is marvelously scented. It looks especially beautiful with any blue flower, here an eryngium. Others include catmint, agastache, baptisia, and any number of veronicas.

Bouquets

SEEN IN VASES, ALL ROSES SOLICIT A SIGH. Some are fleeting while others last a week or more. The cool of the day is the best time for cutting, when buds are unfurling or flowers are newly opened. Plunge in room temperature water and change the water daily to prolong flower life.

Among the earliest cultivated roses recommended for cutting are the apothecary's rose and 'Rosa Mundi.' Other gallicas to cut include 'Camaieux,' 'Duc de Guiche,' 'Tricolore de Flandre,' and 'Tuscany Superb.' Centifolias of note for cutting are 'Petite Orleanaise' and 'Tour de Malakoff.' Common moss (known before 1700) and 'Chapeau de Napoléon' or crested moss also make a satisfactory cut. Recommended Portlands for cutting are 'Comte de Chambord' and 'Jacques Cartier.' Albas also of note are 'Felicité Parmentier,' 'Konigin von Danemark,' and 'Mme Plantier.'

The same as when cutting bouquets of tea roses, the effect of the act on old roses amounts to pruning: Usually it's smart to cut about a quarter inch above a healthy leaf at the base of which is a promising bud facing out from the center of the bush.

OPPOSITE & LEFT: Old and recent roses are an effortless combination in large or small bouquets. Add ripe seed hips for extra color.

57

OPPOSITES ATTRACT

BLUE AND YELLOW *are opposites on the color wheel, so it is no wonder we feel certain contentment in the presence of blue skies and yellow roses. We can capture this elusive state by placing cut roses such as 'Graham Thomas' in cobalt-blue bottles.*

'Graham Thomas,' David Austin's 1983 English rose, honors Graham Stuart Thomas who turned the modern world on to the old shrub roses in the 1960s. In 1972 Thomas created a rose garden in Hampshire in the south of England at Mottisfont Abbey in what in the 12th century had been the kitchen garden. Today it is a vision of paradise to each visitor.

'Graham Thomas' is the quintessential modern shrub rose. It is vigorous, everblooming, and fragrant. Since the canes can exceed 10 feet, self-pegging is recommended: Tie the tip of one cane to a lower one to get bouquets of roses on every lateral, plenty for garden effect and to cut for the house.

Bourbons for cutting include 'Adam Messerich,' 'Coquette des Blanches,' 'La Reine Victoria,' 'Louise Odier,' and 'Mme. Pierre Oger.' Noisettes favored for cutting are 'Mme. Alfred Carrière,' 'Marechal Niel,' and 'Rêve d'Or.'

Top cut teas include 'Maman Cochet' and 'Snowflake.' The hybrid perpetual 'American Beauty' was introduced originally in 1875 as a florist rose.

To make potpourri, harvest the most fragrant roses in the cool of day when they are opening or in their prime. To dry, scatter the petals in a single layer on a screen or several layers of newspaper in an airy place.

Even multiflora rose hips, gathered from the wild, are pretty in fall and winter decorations. However, more spectacular hips are produced by *Rosa elegantula* 'Persetosa' (formerly *Rosa farreri* 'Persetosa'; also called Farrer's threepennybit rose), *R. moyesii* and its variety 'Geranium,' *R. villosa* (formerly *R. pomifera*), *R. eglanteria,* and *R. glauca* (formerly *R. rubrifolia*). Rose hips look cheerful bunched alone or mixed with fresh-cut evergreens.

ABOVE: This collection of old roses includes *Rosa viridiflora,* from China circa 1830. This unusual green rose is a favorite of arrangers. AT RIGHT: It takes only a half dozen bushes to have roses at your door to greet visitors (and yourself) as well as for an arrangement for the house or to give a friend.

RESOURCES

Some North American Rosebush Suppliers & Specialists

Bridges Roses
2734 Toney Road
Lawndale, NC 28090
704.538.9412; catalog $1

W. Atlee Burpee & Co.
300 Park Ave.
Warminster, PA 18974-0001
800.333.5808; catalog free

Butner's Old Mill Nursery
806 South Belt Highway
St. Joseph, MO 64507
816.279.7434; catalog free

Carroll Gardens, Inc.
444 East Main Street
P.O. Box 310, Westminster, MD 21158
410.848.5422; catalog $3

Donovan's Roses
P.O. Box 37800
Shreveport, LA 71133-7800
318.861.6693; catalog for SASE

Hardy Roses of the North
Box 9
Danville, WA 99121-0009
250.442.8442

Hidden Springs Nursery
170 Hidden Springs Lane
Cookeville, TN 38501;
catalog $1

Historical Roses
1657 West Jackson Street
Painesville, OH 44077
216.357.7270 (SASE for catalog)

Hortico, Inc.
723 Robson Rd.
Waterdown, ON L0R 2H1
Canada 905.689.6984;
catalog $3

Interstate Nurseries
1706 Morrissey Drive
Bloomington, IL 61704

Jackson & Perkins Co.
1 Rose Lane
Medford, OR 97501
1.800.USA.ROSE

Kelly Nurseries
410 8th Ave. N.W.
Faribault, MN 55021
507.334.1623

Louisiana Nursery
Route 7, Box 43
Opelousas, LA 70570
318.948.3696; catalog $6

Lowe's Own-Root Roses
6 Sheffield Road
Nashua, NH 03062;
catalog $2

Mini-Rose Garden
P.O. Box 203
Cross Hill, SC 29332
864.998.4331

Moore Sequoia Nursery
2519 E. Noble
Visalia, CA 83282
209.732.0190; catalog free

Nor'East Miniature Roses, Inc.
P.O. Box 307
Rowley, MA 01969
508.948.7964

Northland Rosarium
9405 S. Williams Lane
Spokane, WA 99224
E-mail cparton@ior.com

Park Seed
Cokesbury Road
Greenwood, SC 29647-0001
864.223.7333

Pickering Nurseries, Inc.
670 Kingston Road
Pickering, Ont. L1V 1A6
Canada
905.839.2111; catalog $4

Plants of the Southwest
Aqua Fria, Route 6,
Box 11A
Santa Fe, NM 87501;
catalog $3.50

Rose Acres
6641 Crystal Boulevard
El Dorado, CA 95623-4804
916.626.1722

Roseraie at Bayfields, The
P.O. Box R
Waldoboro, ME 04572
207.832.6330;
narrated video catalog $9

Roses & Wine
3528 Montclair Road
Cameron Park, CA 95682
916.677.9722

Spring Hill Nurseries
110 W. Elm Street
Tipp City, OH 45371

Spring Valley Roses
N7637 330th Street
P.O. Box 7
Spring Valley, WI 54767
715.778.4481

Wayside Gardens
1 Garden Lane
Hodges, SC 29695-0001
800.845.1124

White Flower Farm
P.O. Box 50
Litchfield, CT 06759-0050
800.503.9624; catalog $4

Rose Society and Competitions

American Rose Society
P.O. Box 3900
Shreveport, LA 71130-0030
318.938.5402

All-America Rose Selections, Inc.
221 N. LaSalle St., Suite 3900
Chicago, IL 60601
312.372.7090

Metric Conversions
APPROXIMATE

TEMPERATURE				LENGTH		
WHEN YOU KNOW	MULTIPLY BY	TO FIND		WHEN YOU KNOW	MULTIPLY BY	TO FIND
°F / Fahrenheit temp.	5/9 (-32)	Celsius temp. / c°		in. / inches	2.54	centimeters / CM
°C / Celsius temp.	9/5 (+32)	Fahrenheit temp. / F°		ft. / feet	30	centimeters / CM